Tynemouth Priory, Castle and Twentieth-Century Fortifications

TYNE AND WEAR

ANDREW SAUNDERS MA, FSA, FRHistS

The present grassed emptiness of the interior is misleading and gives a false perspective. In the Middle Ages, when the priory and castle flourished, the headland was full of buildings - the claustral ranges of the monks, the accommodation for guests and pilgrims, and the barns and agricultural structures which provided the economic and subsistence basis for the priory. In addition, there would have been domestic and administrative buildings associated with the castle.

Long after the priory had been dissolved, military occupation continued into recent times when the soldiers' barracks, huts, magazines, and store buildings were swept away and the interior was put down to grass.

The prominent headland, immediately north of the River Tyne, has a long and varied history. This handbook takes you on a tour of the priory, castle and twentieth-century fortifications, explains how the buildings and their uses changed over the centuries, and tells the history of the site, which gives an understanding of the lives of those who lived and worked there. The illustration above shows a window in the Percy Chantry.

ENGLISH HERITAGE · LONDON

Contents

*Published by English Heritage
23 Savile Row London W1S 2ET*
© *Copyright English Heritage 1993
First published 1993, reprinted 1999, 2001, 2002, 2004
Printed in England by The Colourhouse*
C30, 8/04, 04249
ISBN 1 85074 410 6

Introduction

Lighthouse, east end of the priory church and the castle gatehouse on the headland

'. . . a dainty-seated castle almost compassed with the sea, wherein hath been the fairest church I have seen in any castle, but it is now out of repair and much neglected. . . .'
SIR WILLIAM BRERETON, 1635

The prominent headland, immediately north of the River Tyne, has a long and varied history. This bold and windswept rock outcrop has survived in an eroding coastline and this has given it significant defensive qualities. Its high cliffs of sandstone and magnesium limestone give natural advantages. There is only a narrow neck of land connecting the promontory with its hinterland. This neck has been cut off by a deep man-made ditch and earth bank, perhaps from as early as prehistoric times. In the sixteenth century the promontory was still known as Penbal Crag, or 'the head of the rampart on the rock,' but the name Tynemouth was in use during the Anglo-Saxon period.

From the headland, shipping approaching the Tyne can be seen for a great distance as can the coastline to north and south. It is, however, separated from the north bank of the river by a smaller and lower promontory (Spanish Battery), with the small Prior's Haven in between. The latter has given a protected landing place for those occupying the headland but the lower promontory, until recent times, has denied them direct control of the river mouth.

Tynemouth has produced some evidence for Iron Age and Roman activity but the Roman fort controlling the mouth of the river is on the low hill of The Lawe at South Shields on the opposite bank. It would not be surprising if there had been some form of Roman military presence at Tynemouth, perhaps in the form of a signal station which could have communicated with the fort at South Shields from where visibility was much more restricted, but no evidence has so far come to light.

3

The headland was certainly the site for one of the early Christian monasteries in seventh-century Northumbria and achieved fame by being the burial place of St Oswin, formerly King of Deira. Its situation, however, was not sufficient protection from Danish raiders and it was burnt in the year 800. The monastic tradition survived so that after the Norman Conquest the present Benedictine priory was refounded but as a dependency of St Albans Abbey.

The long-standing defensive qualities of the site were such that the priory developed within a castle enclosure, a necessity provoked by the insecurity of the border region between Scotland and England in which raiding and more formal warfare were prevalent during the Middle Ages. When the monastery's active life ended in 1539, the site became part of Henry VIII's scheme of national defence and the fortifications were extended across the front of both headlands to include what was later to be called Spanish Battery. By the early twentieth century, Tynemouth was the controlling hub of the Tyne Defences which extended along the coast from Blyth in the north to the batteries south of Sunderland.

There has also been a long history at Tynemouth of navigational aids and life saving. The medieval monastery church carried a light as a guide to mariners, to be replaced in the seventeenth century by a purpose-built lighthouse, and its successor remained until its demolition in 1898. Nearby, in front of the Collingwood Monument on the lower promontory to the south, the watchhouse of the Tynemouth Volunteer Life Brigade (the first of its kind in the country) is still in being and contains a museum to life saving in the Tyne. The construction of the two great piers by the Tyne Commissioners, protecting the mouth of the river and the dredging of the river

channel, should also be mentioned as an improvement to navigation. The present regional headquarters of the Coastguard beside the priory ruins is merely the most recent development in this cause.

All of these factors - monastic, military, and navigational - have left their mark on the headland. Yet the long period of later military occupation from the sixteenth century to 1960 was very destructive of the medieval buildings, and the subsequent removal of unsightly military structures has had its effect by virtually eliminating another historical dimension. Neither priory, castle, nor even the twentieth-century gun batteries remain in anything like completeness. It is a fragmented picture.

The ruins of the priory now mainly represent the first Norman church of St Mary and St Oswin, and then its enlargement in the early thirteenth century, which now provides its principal architectural and monumental quality. The castle is dominated by its late fourteenth-century gatehouse. The modern concrete gun batteries and the magazines beneath are among the last vestiges of British coastal fortification and among the best preserved of their period.

The present grassed emptiness of the interior is misleading and gives a false perspective. In the Middle Ages, when the priory and castle flourished, the headland was full of buildings - the claustral ranges of the monks, the accommodation for guests and pilgrims, and the barns and agricultural structures which provided the economic and subsistence basis for the priory. In addition, there would have been domestic and administrative buildings associated with the castle. Long after the priory had been dissolved, military occupation continued into recent times until the soldiers barracks, huts, magazines, and store buildings were swept away and the interior put down to grass.

Descriptive Tour

Priory church, looking southeast. The west front of the church is in the foreground with the magnificent east end rising beyond to almost its original height

Having passed through the gatehouse, the most distinctive structure on the headland is the priory church. To the right (south) of it are the low walls providing the outline of the monastic buildings around the cloister (see the plan on pages 22-23 and the aerial view inside the front cover). Beyond the towering east end of the priory church, towards the edge of the headland, is the twentieth-century coastal gun battery with its restored underground magazines.

Returning towards the gatehouse entrance, the descriptive tour turns to the defences of the castle and the gatehouse itself. The outer defences are best appreciated on leaving the castle.

THE PRIORY
Priory church

A church which has been in use for hundreds of years usually shows signs of rebuilding and alterations which conformed to the particular architectural styles of the time. At Tynemouth there are two main phases: the first from the thirty or so years beginning about 1090, and the second coming with the enlargement of the Norman church about a century later from about 1195 to 1220 in a characteristically northern Early English style.

It is possible to reconstruct in the mind the elements of the first Norman church. Much of the aisled nave is distinguishable

5

Doorway with five orders and decorated hoodmould, and, to the right, trefoil-arched niches in the west front of the priory church

and the ground plan of the eastern end has been marked out in the grass following excavation (refer to the plan on page 22). The church was cruciform in plan with a tower over the crossing between the eastern arm or presbytery, the north and south transepts, and the nave to the west.

Much of the eastern bay of the northern aisle of the Norman nave, with the arched opening into the north transept, survives as it was included in a walled chamber relating to the use of the church after the priory was suppressed. In the north wall are portions of a single semicircular-headed window, suggesting that this was the pattern for the nave as a whole. One complete circular aisle pier, with an arcaded capital remains with a blocked arch of two orders (see *Glossary*). This carried a triforium arcade, the east jamb of which can still be seen. In the

corresponding bay of the south aisle are the jambs of two gallery openings and the blocked head of a round-headed opening to the east.

Three of the tower crossing piers remain complete with their weathered scalloped capitals. To the east only the outline of the former presbytery appears marked out in the grass. This indicates an apsidal east end with a processional way or ambulatory inside it, and three projecting apsidal chapels. There were also single apsidal chapels on the eastern side of the transepts. This type of plan, of French origin, is associated with such major English abbeys as Battle and St Augustine's (Canterbury) and is typically Benedictine.

This first church had a comparatively short nave of seven bays and the position of its demolished west wall can be seen in the scars in the north and south walls, two bays from the present west end. An idea of the external elevation of the nave can be gained from the series of pilaster buttresses along its north wall. The early nave was extended by a further two bays about 1220, presumably because of an increasing number of layfolk using the nave as a parish church.

The later west front of the church was highly elaborate. The central doorway (the arch nearest to the castle) is recessed behind five moulded orders with the capitals over detached shafts. Above the arch is a hoodmould decorated with dog-tooth ornament. On either side of the door is blind arcading: three bays to the south and four to the north. Oddly, the arches on either side of the door have unequal width. At a higher level, on the south side, are two trefoil-headed niches,

presumably for statues. Higher still are the remains of a corbel table and an upper tier of pointed blind arcading raked upwards towards the gable. On the northern angle are traces of an octagonal turret.

These architectural fragments point to a unity of design with the great east end of the presbytery. The architectural concept was here destroyed early in the fifteenth century by the insertion of a large seven-light window and another window to the north which removed the arcading. To the south, the west front was further disturbed by the insertion of arches which connected it with a tower built alongside in the fourteenth century. Some massive foundations for this tower remain a short distance to the west. It was known as the Little Tower, perhaps a belfry, but was also referred to as the Hye Prison in the sixteenth century (see the plan, page 22).

Looking east from the nave with the rood screen and crossing beyond

East end of the church seen through the arch into the south quire aisle

The aisles of the nave were vaulted. A doorway on the north side of the westernmost bay appears to lead to a porch. A door further east connected the parish priest's house with the nave. In the northeast bay a single-light Norman window has been replaced by one with a double ogee head. This bay is now enclosed by later walls. Inside are two large stone coffins.

Presbytery

The glory of the ruins is the presbytery, begun in the 1190s and still standing 73 feet (22m) to nearly its full height. This projected from a five-bay aisled quire to the west (of which little remains) which had replaced the Norman quire on a very much grander scale.

The parochial nave was now separated from the monks' quire by a stone wall known as a rood screen, so-called from the cross (rood) and imagery of the Crucifixion which were formerly set above it. The wall has two round-headed

moulded doorways at either end, and blank arcading in the middle of the eastern side. One bay of the south aisle of the thirteenth-century quire remains. The arch has three outer orders with detached shafts. A fragment of diagonal vault rib demonstrates the treatment of the additional south transept and also the aisle.

The presbytery consists of four bays. The east wall, with its three long lancet windows, a middle stage with a central pointed oval or vesica-shaped window and small lancets on either side and above that a single central lancet, is an unusual composition for England and is paralleled by some of the eastern Scottish churches such as Arbroath Abbey and Dunblane. The prominently projecting presbytery is also a northern characteristic to be seen at Arbroath Abbey, St Andrew's Cathedral, and Jedburgh Abbey in Scotland, and at Lanercost Priory in Cumbria.

Internally, the walls of the presbytery are divided into three stages of unequal height, with a later chamber added over the vault. The lowest stage has a blank wall arcade resting on a plinth. This arcade has been cut for later tomb recesses in the easternmost bay but in the south wall incorporates an aumbry (cupboard) and a trefoil-headed piscina (basin) for the service of an altar, and a double sedilia (stone seats for the priests). In the centre of the east wall was a wide arch for a reredos (screen), which was later converted to a doorway into the Percy Chantry (see page 11) with bearded heads in the spandrels of a four-centred arch.

The second and main element of the wall elevations was divided into tall bays separated by clusters of attached shafts. The vaulting sprang from the capitals of the shafts in a quadripartite form. At the east end there were two additional vault ribs. Within each of the three eastern bays

Interior of the south wall of the presbytery. Below the lancet windows is a blank wall arcade with a tomb recess, aumbry (cupboard), piscina (basin) and selilia (priests' seats)

was a tall lancet window with two shafts in the jambs. There is dog-tooth ornament freely applied to the arches, to the horizontal string course of the east wall and between the vaulting ribs.

In the south wall there is a second tier of windows at the springing of the vault. The western bay is treated differently. It is

Interior of the magnificent east wall, with the door to the Percy Chantry

narrower, without windows, and links with the quire. At the level of the quire triforium is an opening with a pair of pointed arches beneath a semi-circular arch. A doorway at floor level gives on to spiral stairs within the wall, which serve the wall passages at each level of the presbytery and an upper chamber which was added in the fourteenth or fifteenth century.

The upper chamber was built over the vaulting of the presbytery and was lit by

A window in the Percy Chantry

topped by octagonal spires.

Later in the fourteenth or fifteenth century, when the upper chamber was added, the gable was raised and the original proportions were destroyed. High on the exterior of the south wall is a carved corbel table.

Percy Chantry

Projecting from the east end of the church is a small vaulted chapel of the fifteenth century, the so-called Percy Chantry. This is the only complete element of the church (though much restored), and it survives with its low heavy vault and elaborately carved bosses. The design of the interlacing rib-vault is very ingenious, with diagonal, longitudinal and transverse ridge ribs. The scheme of the vaulting, with an identification of the roof bosses, is on page 13.

The tracery of the rose window in the east wall is of the nineteenth-century

large traceried windows, two of which remain on the south side and by the earlier lancet (tall narrow window) high in the east wall. There is no record of its use. It could have provided additional altars but access to it was always restricted; it could have served as a muniment room (i.e. a room for storing important documents). A similar upper chamber existed at Brinkburn Priory, some 25 miles to the northwest.

The magnificent vertical composition of the east wall of the presbytery can best be appreciated from outside. The single upper lancet window has stepped blank arcading with pointed arches on shafts with moulded caps and bases on either side following the pitch of the roof. The lines of the original gable can be seen, with slender octagonal turrets enriched with angle shafts at each corner of the east wall. The turrets were originally hollow in their upper stages and may have been

Exterior of the east wall of the presbytery showing the fine vertical composition. The Percy Chantry is below

restoration. Beside it are figures of an angel and the Virgin Mary depicting the Annunciation. The empty niches on either side of the reredos recess would have held other sculptured figures. Whether the chapel was a chantry is open to doubt, though the association with the Percy family is clear. It is in the traditional

The Percy Chantry

EAST END

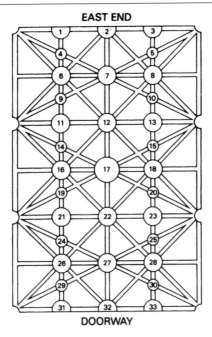

DOORWAY

Roof bosses

1 Eagle of St John holding scroll (broken)
2 Head of Christ
3 Angel of St Matthew holding scroll
4 IHS under a crown
5 Square rose
6 St John the Evangelist seated holding palm leaf (r) and book
7 The risen Christ holding banner, small figure of St Mary Magdalene below
8 St James the Less seated holding fuller's bat (r) and book
9 M, the monogram of the Virgin
10 Emblems of the Crucifixion: crown of thorns, cross, three nails and hammer
11 St Philip seated holding three leaves (r) and book
12 St Andrew seated
13 St Thomas seated holding book (r) and spear
14 Star with nine rays
15 Circular rose
16 St Paul seated holding sword (r) and book, with a head under a cushion at his feet

17 Christ seated between four angels with trumpets
18 St Peter seated holding keys (r) and book, with a head under a cushion at his feet
19 Sun encircled by IHVS MERCY
20 Bearded head
21 St Bartholomew seated holding book (r) and flaying knife
22 St James seated holding staff (r) and book
23 St Matthew seated holding book (r) and saw
24 Percy crescent and shackle bolt on shield
25 Monogram of Prior John Langton
26 St Symon seated holding book (r) and pillar
27 St John the Baptist holding lamb
28 St Thaddeus seated holding book (r) and halberd
29 Monogram of Prior John Langton
30 Emblems of the five wounds of Christ
31 Lion of St Mark holding scroll
32 Lamb of God with cross and flag
33 Ox of St Luke holding scroll

East end of the priory church and the Percy Chantry, looking southwest over the Tyne

position for a Lady Chapel though the site of a chapel on the north side of the presbytery and projecting one bay farther east is thought to be the Lady Chapel begun about 1326 by Prior Richard de Tewing.

Monastic buildings

As was customary, the principal monastic buildings were grouped on three sides of a square open cloister garth, here placed against the south side of the church nave, with covered alleys connecting them. Little survives above ground level but the arrangement of the main individual elements can be recognised. The early twelfth-century layout was broadly retained though the claustral ranges were much rebuilt in later centuries and greatly mutilated during military use of the site. Moving clockwise round the **cloister** (see the plan on page 22), the **chapter house** abutted the south transept of the

church. This was where the daily business of the priory was carried out. It was rebuilt in the mid thirteenth century after the completion of the quire aisles. The column bases for an elaborate west door remain and a wall arcade providing seats for the monks is on the north side. Stairs to the dormitory on an upper floor are next to the chapter house.

The **warming house** (note the floor tiles which are a rare survival in northern England) was the only room in a monastery, apart from the kitchen, where a fire was allowed. This occupied the rest of the eastern side of the cloister, with a small parlour to its north beside the stairs, and a passage (slype) separating it from the complex of buildings occupied by the prior stretching down the slope to the south.

On the first floor of the east range was the **dormitory** (dorter), and projecting from it at right angles was the latrine block or reredorter (i.e. to the rear of the dorter). Along the south side of the cloister was the **dining hall** (frater or refectory) of which little now remains. On its south wall projects a large multangular buttress which probably served as the base of the pulpit from which readings from the scriptures were given during meals. The **kitchen** seems to have been towards the southwest.

The **west range** was traditionally given over to the cellarer, responsible for the material needs of the community. The ground floor was vaulted and probably used for storage. This range was rebuilt in the thirteenth century.

Against the south wall of the church was the **parlour** which provided communication for the brethren with the outside world. There is a blocked doorway connecting it with the nave and blind arcading on either side of it. There are signs of an outer porch which may have been related to the Little Tower.

Prior's lodgings and adjoining buildings

South of the cloister is a complex of buildings which formed the prior's lodgings. The prior's hall seems to have been a continuation of the east range, five vaulted bays long, later sub-divided by a cross wall. At the south end are two large blocked mid fourteenth-century windows and traces of the rib vaulting.

To the east and at right angles to the hall was the **prior's chapel** of two vaulted bays with two lancet windows on the south. It was later used as a military magazine and considerably altered. It now contains a collection of carved stones from the priory buildings.

The prior's lodging connected to the main drainage system of the **monks' reredorter** which discharged down the cliff to the south. This building is extremely complex with wall after wall

Prior's chapel

wrapped round and inside the original twelfth-century enclosed pit. The impression is one of chronic instability requiring more and more support because the main drainage of the priory was concentrated at this point.

Further to the east are foundations that are presumed to belong to the monastic **infirmary.** The understanding of this complex of walls is made more difficult because of the slope of the ground as well as the extensive military disturbance. The southernmost rooms are 30 feet (nearly 10m) lower than the floor of the nave.

To the west of the prior's hall is another range along the cliff edge that was described as the **New Hall** on a sixteenth-century map and was possibly guest accommodation.

The Monk's Stone

East of the claustral ranges and near the later burial ground is a ninth-century cross shaft set up in the priory ruins but originally coming from a site about 2 miles away. The carving is much weathered and difficult to identify. There are traces of stylised animals with coiled-back heads and tree scroll. Interlaced ornament is the most distinctive motif.

Burial ground

The ruins of the priory church were used as a burial ground for the parish from the seventeenth century onwards, and the site of the monks' cemetery to the south and east of the church continued as an undefined secular burial place despite the removal of the parish church itself to North Shields in 1668.

There are nearly 700 gravestones, mainly covering the period 1715 to 1856 though there were later burials. Many of the inscriptions on the headstones and memorials have weathered to anonymity but there are many of interest. A particular local form is the adoption of table tombs supported by fat baluster legs. On the southern edge is a memorial to Corporal Alexander Rollo whose fame was to have held the lantern at the burial of Sir John Moore at Corunna in 1809 during the Peninsular War.

TWENTIETH-CENTURY COASTAL BATTERY

The cliffs of the headland were adapted for gun batteries during the eighteenth and nineteenth centuries. These were brought up to date, first with breech-loading guns in 1893, and then more substantially in 1902-04. This battery remained operational during both world wars. Beneath the now-empty concrete gun-emplacements are the magazines which served them.

Vital elements of the battery are missing. To make space for the present Coastguard station, the following were all demolished: the Fire Command Observation Post of 1916 (which co-ordinated all the Tyne Harbour Defences from Blyth in the north, to Roker, south of Sunderland), the former c1893 Position-Finding Cell and Fire Command Post, the First World War Admiralty Signal Station, and the 1911 Battery Commander's and Electric Light Detector Post.

By 1914, the armament consisted of one 9.2 inch gun Mark X on a Mark V mounting with a range of 12 000 yards (11 km) for counter-bombardment against large warships. Two 6 inch Mk VII guns on CP Mk I mountings were for close defence and as an examination battery for checking all ships approaching the Tyne. To the southwest, overlooking the river, there were positions for two 12-pounder quick-firing guns to counter fast-moving torpedo boats but these guns were removed by about 1910. Immediately north of the 9.2 inch position, is an emplacement for one of the breech-loading guns of 1893, originally on hydro-pneumatic `disappearing' mountings. Its gun pit is now filled by a Second World War concrete store building but a nearby inscription relates to the magazine of the 6 inch 5 ton breech-loading gun Mk VI.

Just visible at Spanish Battery, on the lower headland beyond Prior's Haven, are the now-filled-up concrete gun-pits for two more 6 inch guns and two 6 pounder quick-firers. There were also positions for Defence Electric Lights (searchlights) of about 1912 at the foot of the cliff, one at the junction with the north pier, and there were corresponding lights on the South Shields side of the Tyne.

9.2 inch gun emplacement

The 9.2 inch (233mm) gun was mounted in a deep open-backed concrete position, which required hydraulic power. On the

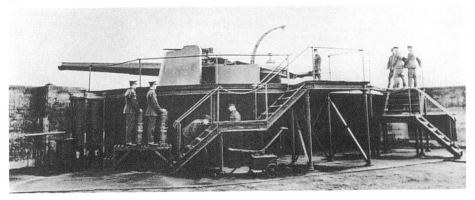

9.2 inch gun on MkV mounting

left side of the emplacement is an open space, roofed over with a sheet of armour plate; this housed the generating engine for the hydraulic power system with the accumulator and tank.

Fifteen men were required to operate the gun and additional men were needed when the ammunition supply was from the magazine below. Stairs lead down to the magazine below the gun emplacement. To the left of the stairs are the gun stores and there is a stand-by watch shelter.

6 inch gun emplacements

Immediately to the south are the concrete emplacements for two 6 inch (152mm) MkVII guns with a range of 12 000 yards (11km). Within a raised concrete wall, behind each D-shaped concrete apron at the level of the earth bank, was a steel ring at floor level on which the gun was mounted. In the sides of the gun pits were the ready-use lockers for both carriage and shell, each closed by steel doors. At the side of each gun pit were the exits of the cartridge hoists from the magazines below. The shells emerged from separate hoists, behind the gun, which are covered by steel hatches.

The standard detachment for a 6 inch

gun MkVII was thirteen men including the ammunition detail in the magazine below. The guns could be fired with open sights but at night or against an invisible target the range and bearing was transmitted by dials from the Battery Observation Post. Between the two gun positions were two 'Lying Down Shelters' (each for six men) for the gun detachments on duty.

6 inch gun magazines

The magazines for housing reserve ammunition for the two 6 inch guns have been restored, with such details as the ventilators above. There are explanatory

Shell hoist in the magazine below the six-inch gun battery

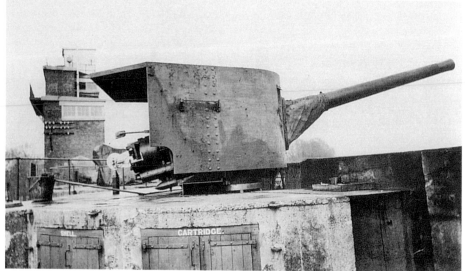

6 inch gun Mk7 on CP Mk2 mounting

exhibitions. (The magazines for the 9.2 inch gun, the two quick-firers and that for the 1893 six-inch gun are not yet open to the public.)

Within the magazines great care had to be taken to avoid a catastrophe. The charges and projectiles were always stored separately and the magazines are arranged in two parts to limit the risk of explosion. The long outer chamber was for shells and an inner wall separated it from the cartridge store which was subject to stringent regulations. It was divided into `dirty' and `clean' areas and was entered through a shifting lobby. Anyone entering the cartridge store had to put on special canvas shoes and clothing to avoid the risk of sparks.

The benches, clothes hooks and the lifting barrier of the shifting lobby have been restored according to the War Office specifications. So have the wooden racks for storing the cartridges.

When needed for action the prepared cartridges were passed through the low issue-hatches at either end of the store for placing in the cartridge hoist and raising to the gun-pit above. In the shell store the shells stood on boards until they were fused and raised to the gun on the separate shell ladder hoists. The magazines were lit by special candle lamps in glazed lamp recesses. There was a lamp store at the south end of the magazines with a small shelter alongside for the stand-by watch, equipped with hammock hooks and a fireplace. At the opposite end was an artillery store for keeping such things as sights, elevating arcs and various removable fittings. On the wall at the rear of the battery were folding benches

Six-inch gun battery, looking south

and a rifle rack which have recently been replaced.

The two 12-pounder quick-firers were on octagonal concrete bases and low concrete aprons in front. The circular rings of six holdfasts show how the mountings were fixed. The magazine was to the left. There are also two open-fronted brick-vaulted casemates for accommodation. They would originally have been closed by wooden frames with doors and windows, and equipped with hammock hooks, rifle racks, trestle tables, benches, and some clothes pegs.

Coastguard station

The Coastguard Station is no longer operational. It stands on the site of the Fire Command buildings. A survival from the earlier lighthouse period is a short length of wall containing a gateway with a pedimented top.

On the earth bank between the 6 inch gun emplacements and the quick-firer battery, a heliograph was situated within an iron fenced enclosure for recording the sun's activities. This was on the site of a former lookout across the mouth of the Tyne and, more recently, an emplacement of about 1940 for a 4 inch naval gun, primarily for the training of the crews of defended merchant ships.

THE CASTLE AND OTHER FORTIFICATIONS

During the Middle Ages there was a continuous wall with towers around the headland. This line of defence has largely gone along the south side because of quarrying and natural erosion. The present wall along the northern cliff edge is thin with loop holes (narrow vertical slits) and is comparatively recent in date. At a lower level, above the beach to the northwest, are the ruins of the square Whitley Tower, which was more than three storeys high.

On the northern cliff edge is a coast defence 6 inch muzzle-loading gun of 1859, which now commemorates the centenary of the Tynemouth Volunteer Artillery 1859-1959.

General Sir Allan Brooke inspecting men of 508 Coast Regiment

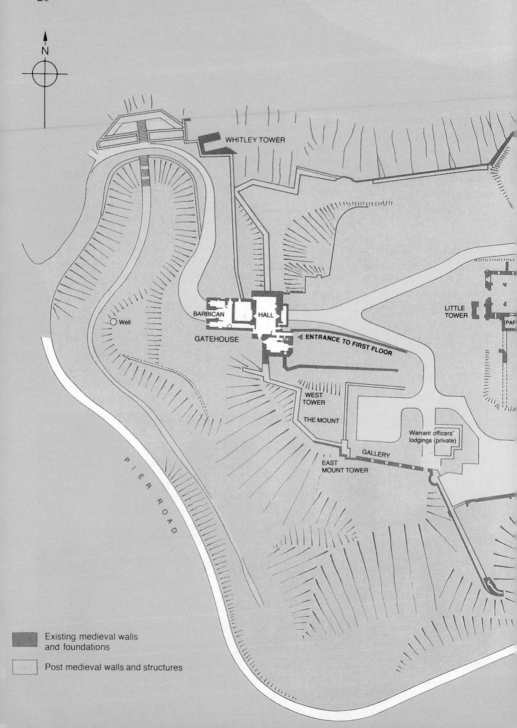

N

WHITLEY TOWER

BARBICAN HALL

GATEHOUSE

Well

ENTRANCE TO FIRST FLOOR

LITTLE TOWER

PAP

WEST TOWER

THE MOUNT

Warrant officers' lodgings (private)

GALLERY

EAST MOUNT TOWER

P I E R   R O A D

Existing medieval walls and foundations

Post medieval walls and structures

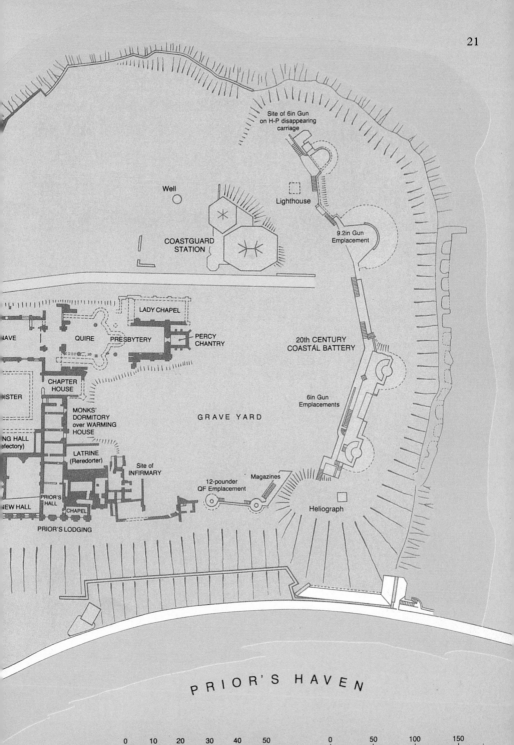

Site of 6in Gun
on H-P disappearing
carriage

Well

Lighthouse

9.2in Gun
Emplacement

COASTGUARD
STATION

LADY CHAPEL

NAVE

QUIRE PRESBYTERY

PERCY
CHANTRY

20th CENTURY
COASTAL BATTERY

CHAPTER
HOUSE

ISTER

MONKS'
DORMITORY
over WARMING
HOUSE

GRAVE YARD

6in Gun
Emplacements

NG HALL
efectory)

LATRINE
(Reredorter)

Site of
INFIRMARY

12-pounder
QF Emplacement

Magazines

PRIOR'S
HALL

NEW HALL

CHAPEL

Heliograph

PRIOR'S LODGING

PRIOR'S HAVEN

0   10   20   30   40   50
Metres

0   50   100   150
Feet

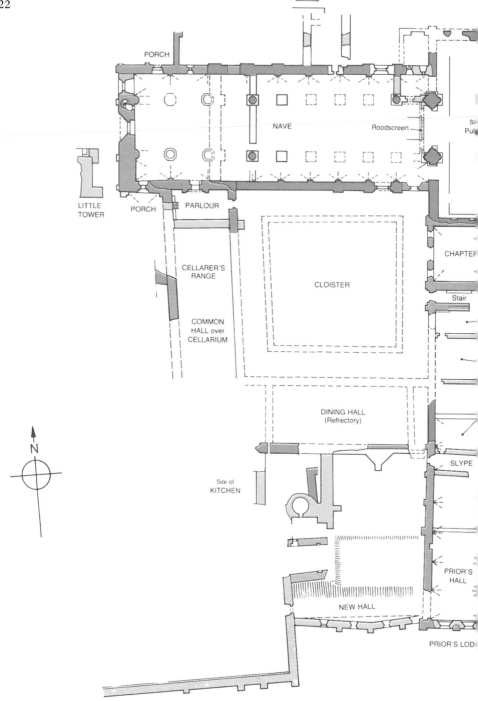

PORCH

NAVE

Roodscreen

Si
Puḷ

LITTLE
TOWER

PORCH

PARLOUR

CELLARER'S
RANGE

CLOISTER

CHAPTEI

Stair

COMMON
HALL over
CELLARIUM

DINING HALL
(Refrectory)

SLYPE

N

Site of
KITCHEN

PRIOR'S
HALL

NEW HALL

PRIOR'S LOD

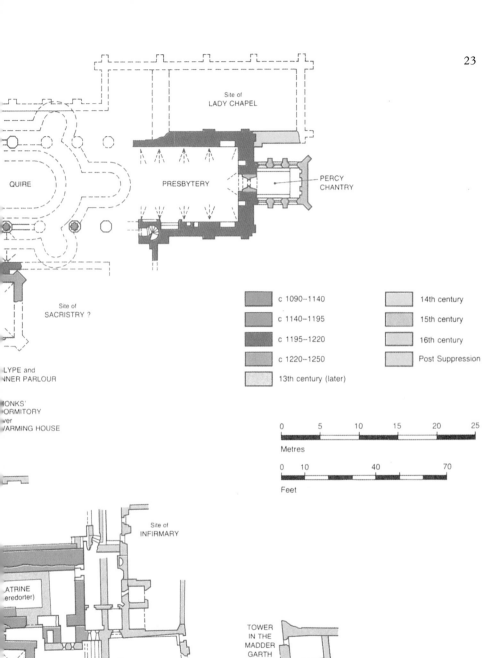

Site of
LADY CHAPEL

QUIRE

PRESBYTERY

PERCY
CHANTRY

Site of
SACRISTRY ?

LYPE and
NNER PARLOUR

ONKS'
ORMITORY
ver
ARMING HOUSE

c 1090–1140	14th century
c 1140–1195	15th century
c 1195–1220	16th century
c 1220–1250	Post Suppression
13th century (later)	

| 0 | 5 | 10 | 15 | 20 | 25 |

Metres

| 0 | 10 | 40 | 70 |

Feet

Site of
INFIRMARY

ATRINE
eredorter)

TOWER
IN THE
MADDER
GARTH

13th
century
drains

HAPEL

Stair

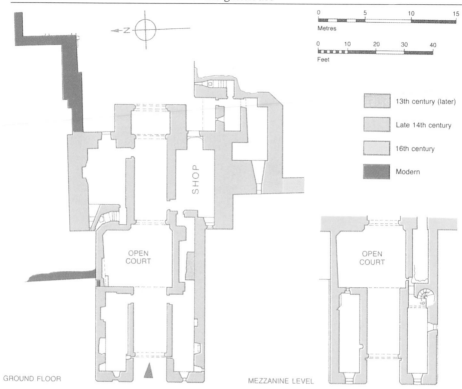

0   5   10   15
Metres

0   10   20   30   40
Feet

13th century (later)

Late 14th century

16th century

Modern

SHOP

OPEN COURT

OPEN COURT

GROUND FLOOR

MEZZANINE LEVEL

Inner side of the gatehouse. The entrance to the first floor is up the grassy slope on the left

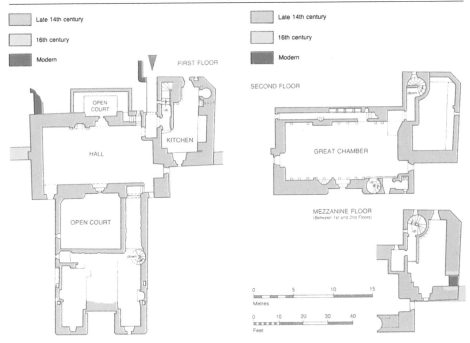

On the southwest side of the castle is rather more medieval walling, commencing with the remains of the East Mount Tower south of the gatehouse, to which is attached a thick loopholed wall labelled The Gallery on the Elizabethan map. A number of sixteenth-century gunports can be found in this stretch. A length of curtain wall runs off at an angle down the cliff with a half-round solid tower, probably dating from the thirteenth century, at its northern end and finishing with a tower-like extension containing stairs above Prior's Haven.

The red-brick house on the south side of the interior, prominently dated 1895, is the last survivor of the many nineteenth- and twentieth-century military buildings occupying the interior. The house was built to house four warrant officers; it is not open to the public.

The dominating gatehouse occupies a central position in the main defences across the neck of the promontory. On either side is a massive earth rampart which initially replaced the medieval curtain wall in the sixteenth century in order to carry artillery. In their present form these ramparts are now revetted in fine masonry and are angled for enfilading fire (covering the length of the wall), with gun platforms and low masonry parapets for the nineteenth-century howitzers.

Undoubtedly this is the primary defence line throughout the castle's history. The earth bank is slightly higher on the south and spreads outwards beyond the general line. It was described as The Mount on the Elizabethan map, and it is quite possible that here was a motte (mound) intended to carry the principal tower of an early Norman castle.

Gatehouse

The principal element of the castle is the gatehouse. It is an elegant tower house with substantial defences in the form of a strong outer barbican in advance of the entrance. This, and a smaller barbican protecting the rear gateway, made possible the total isolation of the gatehouse from the rest of the castle. The design has similarities with gatehouses at Alnwick and Prudhoe Castles.

The present gatehouse is that built by Prior John de Whethamsted in the last years of the fourteenth century and was the last of a succession of gatehouse structures on this spot. Until 1783 it preserved much of its original appearance but then it was extensively altered to convert it for barrack purposes. The resulting brick superstructure over the outer barbican was damaged by fire in 1936 and this was the opportunity to remove its remains and expose what was left of the medieval masonry.

Kitchen with Mount Chamber above. Note the large fireplace, basin and bread oven on the right

First floor

The gatehouse is set over the gate passage and is now approached by way of a grassy slope to a doorway at first-floor level (see the plans and the illustration on page 24) in the side block which contained the kitchen. In the wall face above this doorway is a recess to take a drawbridge (replaced by a modern bridge above the exit from the ticket office and shop).

On entering, there is a small lobby with a flat stone ceiling resting on continuous corbel courses. From the lobby are two doorways. Turn left to an inner lobby; on the left are stairs, and on the right is the kitchen.

The **kitchen** is irregular in shape because the stair turret projects into the northeast corner. Along the south wall is a large fireplace and a bread oven, with a basin in between draining through the wall. Curiously this wall is not bonded into the west wall; nevertheless it is part of the gatehouse in other respects. This suggests that there was an existing curtain wall standing when the kitchen block was built. A chamfered corbel course carried the floor joists of the room above. Below the kitchen are small vaulted chambers only accessible at ground level, but not open to the public.

The other door from the entrance lobby leads to the **hall** (principal room) of the gatehouse. This occupies the space over the gate passage and the ground-floor rooms on either side of it. This was the hall for conducting business and entertaining guests. Food was served from the adjacent kitchen. There are the remains of a large fireplace and a two-light transomed window in the east wall; two similar large windows are in the wall opposite and there is another in the south wall. The doorways in the east and west walls gave access to the barbicans.

Only a little of the medieval arrangements over the outer barbican can

Northwest corner of the hall with the great chamber above

now be seen from this level. There is a spiral staircase on the south side, from the guard chambers below. Bases of windows, rather than arrow loops, and the presence of fireplaces imply some residential use. The open chamber on the south contains a latrine pit which seems to occupy the remains of an early ditch. There is also the suggestion of an earlier east-west wall line extending beneath the later barbican.

Second floor
The great chamber, above the hall, could be reached via the stairs from the inner lobby (see the plan on page 24). These stairs lead first to a landing which originally led to a residential room, above the kitchen but at a lower level than the great chamber. The room (perhaps for a steward or similar official) had a fireplace above that in the kitchen and windows in the end walls. A later, Tudor, doorway in the south wall gave access to the curtain wall. This room seems to have been called Mount Chamber in the sixteenth century.

Continue up the stairs to the level of the great chamber, above the hall. The great chamber was another grand room but more private than that below; it would have served both as a living room and a bedroom. Lack of a floor (originally supported by beams resting on the stone corbels projecting from the east and west walls which you can see clearly from this level) means that this room can also be seen from the hall. It too had a fireplace, but this time in the west wall. There were wide two-light transomed windows and access to a latrine in the southwest corner. A door in the east wall led to the passage (best seen by looking up from the hall) which served the machicolations over the rear barbican; stairs from this passage gave access to a passage through the thickness of the south wall and to the wall walk.

From the doorway to the great chamber you can see, opposite in the west wall, a doorway leading to spiral stairs. These led to the roof and the battlements.

Inner side of the gatehouse showing the machicolations over the gate passage, allowing defenders to drop missiles on anyone trying to force the gates

Gatehouse and outer barbican with the redan and ditch in the foreground and the Mount to the right

It would have been from here that the corbelled-out corner turrets (bartizans), which were recorded by eighteenth-century artists, would have been reached. The lower corbelled courses of the southeast bartizan still remain.

Ground floor

The ground floor of the gatehouse has vaulted rooms on either side of a tunnel-vaulted passage (see the plan on page 25). That on the south is now occupied by the ticket office and shop. It had a fireplace, and a door in the west wall gave access to the latrine chamber on the south side of the open court. Outside the inner exit from the shop is a survival of the nineteenth-century military occupation. The pointed-arched door, which leads to small chambers (not open to the public) below the kitchen, is copper-sheathed with 'M[aster] G[unners] Stores, Reserve

Ammunition Store' painted on it. The vaulted room on the other side (north) of the gate passage has a fireplace, a latrine, and windows at either end. It was probably the porter's lodge.

The unusual **inner barbican** is commanded by machicolations at second-floor level (off the great chamber), allowing the defenders to drop missiles on anyone trying to force the gates. There

Machicolations above the inner gate arch

was a pair of gates on its inner side.
In front (to the west) of the gatehouse
is an open court with high walls on either
side. This is likely to be the site of the
earlier defensive ditch in front of the
previous entrance. The barbican lay
outside it. A relieving arch in the north
wall of the courtyard is also an indicator
for the line of a ditch. There is a small late
doorway here with a grill. On the south
side is the latrine block.

The **outer barbican** had two-storey
guardrooms with fireplaces, on either side
of a tunnel-vaulted entrance. There was a
better standard of accommodation over
the passage (now best seen from the west
window of the great hall) and it was from
that level that the portcullis in front of the
outer gate was controlled. The eighteenth-
century barracks was constructed here
and there is now little surviving detail to
explain the workings of the outer defences.

Looked at from the outside, high up on
the northeast corner of the gatehouse, is a
partly blocked doorway which an
eighteenth-century print shows giving on
to a corbelled gallery. It was reached from
the wall passage off the great chamber.
The line of the north curtain wall appears
in the gatehouse wall, east of the great
chamber window.

Tudor and later defences

On either side of the barbican are much
altered earthworks which partly represent
the drastic remodelling of the main front
in 1545 for artillery and are now revetted
in eighteenth-century ashlar masonry. A
new ditch was contrived beyond these
earthworks. This too has been remodelled
and has an angular outwork (redan) in
front of the entrance. The well at the apex
is probably a survival of the time in the
early Middle Ages when houses of the
town clustered in front of the earlier
gatehouse.

As one leaves the castle, the line of the
Tudor ditch can be seen leading across the
headland to the east of the Collingwood
Monument. This was part of a grandiose
scheme to bring the whole headland into a
larger fortification which included the
defence works known as Spanish Battery.

Gatehouse and barbican looking southeast over the Tyne

History

An engraving of the headland, July 1747

Early settlement

Evidence for early settlement has so far been slight, largely because so little of the interior has been examined archaeologically. Excavations on the headland in 1963, following the removal of the military buildings, have provided evidence for one large Iron Age circular timber-built house to the north of the church, and a smaller circular hut nearby which might be Roman. Romano-British pottery was found in the vicinity but no sign of military works.

The headland does not directly control the Tyne entrance and the Roman fort of South Shields was better sited for this purpose. The Roman inscribed stones

which were found re-used as building material on the north side of the church in the eighteenth century may have been brought from the forts at Wallsend or South Shields.

Anglian monastery

An early Christian monastery was established at Tynemouth by the end of the seventh century. Heribald, a friend of the Venerable Bede who died in 735, was abbot for a time. Traditionally, St Oswin, the murdered King of Deira, was buried here in 651 and this event was to be of the greatest importance for Tynemouth. St Oswin inspired great devotion and many miracles were attributed to him.

St Osred, another murdered King of Northumbria, was also buried at Tynemouth in 792. The monastery was plundered by the Danes in 800 and eventually destroyed in 875. There remained subsequently only a church dedicated to St Mary. It was to here that the relics of St Oswin were formally translated in 1065 having been previously taken to Jarrow for safe keeping.

It is particularly interesting that, during the excavations of 1963, four rectangular timber buildings were discovered. There were no associated finds but it seems likely that they were buildings associated with the Anglian monastery as they were distinctly earlier than the Norman monastic buildings. Other rectangular structures, possibly of similar date, were found in 1980 on the site of the new Coastguard building.

Evidence for the early monastery of a more tangible kind are the decorated fragments of Anglian crosses and grave markers which were re-used as building materials. These are now in the Museum of Antiquities in Newcastle-upon-Tyne. The ninth-century cross shaft, the Monk's Stone, standing to the south of the present cemetery, was found about 2 miles away during the eighteenth century and is now the only visible relic of this early date on the site.

Priory

Robert de Mowbray, Earl of Northumberland, refounded the monastery at Tynemouth in 1085 as a Benedictine priory dependent on St Albans Abbey in Hertfordshire; monks were sent from there to colonise their new daughter house. Tynemouth Priory was the principal dependency of St Albans Abbey, and was of great financial value to its mother house. Tynemouth had an additional use as a place where unruly members of the community could be sent into exile.

It was inevitable that this situation was continually challenged by the monks of Durham in whose hands the earlier church at Tynemouth had been. A quarrel between Mowbray and the Bishop of Durham had led to this unexpected outcome.

The building of the priory church seems to have begun by 1090, and the quire and east end were completed by 1110 for the relics of St Oswin to be translated to the new church. It appears from the *Life of St Oswin* that the pre-Conquest church was still standing after the erection of the Norman quire and lay outside it. Another notable event in these early days was the burial here of King Malcolm III of Scotland following his defeat and death at Alnwick in 1093, but his body was subsequently moved to Dunfermline Abbey.

The buildings around the cloister were also under construction and there is a reference to the dormitory in 1111. There was a degree of expansion with the cloister being extended to the west and the western range being rebuilt about 1140. The dining hall (refectory) was completed by about 1150, when there is a report of a fire in a neighbouring building for housing guests.

The enlargement of the east end of the church at the end of the twelfth century has been attributed to Prior Akarius. The construction of the great four-bay presbytery seems to have been intended as a splendid new setting for the shrine of St Oswin, set behind the high altar in the second bay from the east to judge by the position of the aumbry, piscina and sedilia in the south wall. The shrine was a great object of pilgrimage.

A contemporary description of Tynemouth Priory, and life there early in

The priory church, seen from the northeast, as it may have appeared in the thirteenth century

TERRY BALL

the thirteenth century, comes in a letter from an exiled southerner to a fellow monk at St Albans:

Our house is confined to the top of a high rock and is surrounded by the sea on every side but one. Here is the approach to the monastery through a gate cut out of the rock so narrow that a cart can hardly pass through. Day and night the waves break and roar and undermine the cliff. Thick sea frets roll in wrapping everything in gloom. Dim eyes, hoarse voices, sore throats are the consequence. Spring and Summer never come here. The north wind is always blowing and brings with it cold and snow; or storms in which the wind tosses the salt sea in masses over our buildings and rains it down within the castle. Shipwrecks are frequent. It is great pity to see the numbed crew, whom no power on earth can save, whose vessel, mast swaying and timbers parted, rushes upon rock or reef. No ringdove or nightinggale is here, only grey birds which nest in the rocks and greedily prey on the drowned, whose screaming cry is a token of a coming storm . . . In the Spring the sea air blights the blossoms of the stunted fruit trees, so that you think yourself lucky to find a wizened apple, though it will set your teeth on edge should you try to eat it. See to it, dear brother, that you do not come to this comfortless place. But the church is of wondrous beauty. It has been lately completed. Within it rests the body of the blessed martyr, Oswin, in a silver shrine, magnificently embellished with gold and jewels. He protects the murderers, thieves and seditious persons who fly to him and commutes their punishment to exile. He heals those who no physician can cure. The martyr's protection and the church's beauty furnish us with a bond of unity. We are well off for food, thanks to the abundant supply of fish of which we tire.

Much building work continued during the first half of the thirteenth century. This included the addition of two bays to the west of the Norman church and also more work on the claustral buildings. A Lady Chapel was begun about 1326 by Prior Richard of Tewing on the north side of the presbytery. Prior Thomas de la Mare built substantially after 1346. He removed the shrine of St Oswin to another part of the church (perhaps to the new Lady Chapel) in order to separate pilgrimages from the normal monastic services. Prior de la Mare also rebuilt the dormitory in 1347-49.

It may be that the eastern extension, built in the mid fifteenth century and now known as the Percy Chantry, was a replacement for the Lady Chapel. It is appropriately sited and was certainly known by this title in early references. Nevertheless, there is a clear Percy connection as appears from two of the badges in the vaulting bosses.

The nave served the needs of the parish. A settlement between Durham and St Albans in 1140 meant that vicars were appointed by the prior with the consent of the Abbot of St Albans and were admitted by the Bishop of Durham. A door in the north wall of the nave gave access to the priest's lodging.

Much of the history of the priory is one of continuing quarrels with the Bishops of Durham and of mainly commercial rivalries with the town of Newcastle. There were disputes over properties, the maintenance of the Priory's Liberty, and a striving for economic advantages.

In about 1270 Nicholas Scot, Mayor of Newcastle and at the head of over a hundred armed citizens, attacked the priory's new town of North Shields, burnt the mills and many houses, carried off a shipload of coal and inflicted a loss to the priory of £300.

Tynemouth was one of the wealthier monasteries. Besides the usual endowments of land, the priory exploited the local coal deposits, which had been worked at least as early as the latter part of the thirteenth century, and shipped the product out of the Tyne. The Liberty of Tynemouth comprised all the scattered manors and townships held by the prior and the convent. By the end of the thirteenth century this was an extensive franchise.

There were also tensions caused by the efforts of some priors to obtain independence from St Albans. In 1294 this led to the Abbot of St Albans, John de Berkhamstead, with the support of the Mayor of Newcastle and an armed following, forcing his way into the prior's lodging at midnight and carrying off Prior Walden to St Albans, and appointing a replacement.

The priory needed its revenues, for not only were the priors responsible for maintenance of the castle and a garrison but on many occasions they were required to provide accommodation and hospitality for a succession of notables on route to and from Scotland, and sometimes the King himself. Edward II and Piers Gaveston stayed at the priory, Edward III came in 1335, and later, Richard II.

The priory was dissolved in 1539 with all the other major religious houses. At Prior Blakeney's surrender on 12 January there were, besides himself, fifteen monks. The prior was pensioned off and went to live at his manor of Benwell, materials of value were taken from the priory and St Oswin's shrine was broken up. The priory and its lands were leased to Sir Thomas Hilton.

An Elizabethan survey of the headland of about 1577 provides a detailed description of the various buildings associated with the priory and their functions. Barns and agricultural buildings lay mainly to the north of the church; brewhouses, malt kilns, and lodgings for guests were about the inner court to the west.

Medieval defences

Tynemouth's defences seem to have served as a refuge for local people in the troubled early years of the Norman Conquest. Robert de Mowbray's castle was substantial. Following his rebellion in 1095 against the King, William Rufus, Tynemouth was able to hold out against the King's forces for two months before its capture.

The King went on to besiege Bamburgh, and Mowbray tried to cut William's communications to the south but was forced to retreat to Tynemouth with thirty followers. This time the siege lasted only two days and the earl, severely wounded, sought sanctuary in the church only to be dragged out and condemned to suffer a long imprisonment before entering St Albans Abbey and ending his days as a monk of the abbey he had enriched.

The mound to the south of the gatehouse may have been the motte carrying the principal timber tower of this early castle.

With the establishment of the monastery, within the fortified enclosure, the prior was obliged to maintain the castle at his own cost. The main defences would have been across the neck of the headland and there are indications of early masonry structures in the gatehouse area, but the first documented reference to defences is a licence to crenellate of 1296. This was formal consent from the Crown to fortify, and probably represented a reordering of the existing castle. The site involved one of the largest fortifications in England in terms of wall circumference: 3200 feet (974m).

During the war with Scotland in the early fourteenth century, the castle was garrisoned and provisioned against attack. The Whitley Tower may have been constructed about this time and named after Gilbert of Whitleigh who was the master and supervisor of the royal works at Newcastle Castle in 1356. Prior Richard de Tewing maintained a garrison of eighty armed men within the monastery. In 1346, Ralph de Neville attempted to treat Tynemouth as a royal fortress but this move was frustrated by Prior de la Mare. It led to royal recognition that the prior had the right to exercise sole authority within the walls. In 1349, Tynemouth was described in a royal letter as one of the strongest fortresses in the Marches (Anglo-Scottish borderlands).

The present gatehouse was built by Prior John of Wethamstede in the 1390s, perhaps following the fashion for militarily strong outer gatehouses to monasteries, which can be seen at places such as Bury St Edmunds and St Albans. In its design it seems to be a copy of that at Alnwick Castle, with its barbican separated by an open court from the gatehouse itself. It did, however, represent a contribution to national defence and the King and other prominent northern landholders subscribed over £666 towards its cost. Since there were regular visitations from the Abbots of St Albans, as well as royal and other important personages, who would have expected to be accommodated in suitable style at the priory, the new gatehouse may also have served as a splendid guest suite. Its grand internal arrangements support this hypothesis.

Tudor and later defences

At the Dissolution, the priory's run-down defences lacked any sort of ordnance. Yet the potential of the site as a fortress was appreciated and in 1545 Richard Lee, the military engineer, was sent by the King to make an assessment of it, accompanied by two other engineers: Gian Tommaso Scala and Antonio da Bergamo, 'Italians expert in fortifying.' Lee's opinion was that it is 'a place most apte and nedeful to be

fortyfied . . . none within this realme more.' Tynemouth was no longer regarded as an isolated place of refuge but the main defence of the Tyne.

In 1544 the Earl of Hertford had made Tynemouth a base for the English fleet during the invasion of Scotland. A plan, which still survives, was drawn up which envisaged two enormous 'Italian style' demi-bastions at either end of the wider promontory; the southern demi-bastion occupying the area where the Watch House and the adjacent houses now stand, east of the Collingwood Monument.

In fact, these great bastions were not built; instead a wide ditch with a long irregular rampart and wall with flanking emplacements was dug across the neck of the promontory. In the area of the Spanish Battery was a two-tier platform. This position may have got its name from some Spanish mercenaries quartered here at the time of Hertford's Scottish campaign. At the same time, the medieval walls of the castle were reinforced. The walls on either side of the gatehouse appear to have been replaced by stone-revetted earthworks to provide gun platforms.

The fortifications were armed with cannon and there was a garrison of fifty men. There was, however, a longstanding problem. To control the mouth of the Tyne, the batteries needed to be set low on the headland south of the castle but, in order to accommodate the garrison adequately, the castle and priory buildings, some 600 yards (550m) away, had to be used.

By 1584, there were only ten guns in the fortress and of these a saker and two falcons were placed on the Mount. For the rest of the sixteenth century there is a picture of neglect. There were proposals for refortification in 1625 and Spanish Battery was improved during the Civil War. The parish church in the priory nave was in use as an ordnance store in 1558 and by 1608 was in great decay. The church finally fell into ruin during the Civil War, so Christ Church was built at North Shields and consecrated in 1668. The parish burial ground, however, continued to be on the site of the monastic cemetery, causing much friction between later garrisons and parish officials.

In 1640 the castle was seized and garrisoned by the Scots but returned to royal hands in 1642. It was then held by the Royalists until surrendered to Parliament's Scottish allies in 1644. Thereafter it kept changing hands until it was finally recaptured for Parliament by Sir Arthur Heselrig.

After the Restoration of Charles II, the castle's governor was Colonel Sir Edward Villiers. There were nine guns of assorted sizes, with a master gunner and twenty gunners. In 1663 a warrant was made out to Sir Edward Villiers for £3200 for the repair of the fortifications. What was achieved is unclear but Villiers built himself a house and re-established the priory light by building a lighthouse.

By 1676 the castle was much ruined and there was 'great necessity for erecting a half-moon to cover the gate and for making a half bastion before the south battery.' The engineer, Martin Beckman, provided an estimate for repairs but two years later he succinctly described the position as follows: 'This castle as it is now situated doth not deserve the charge of a garrison, it being not a frontier place, nor doth it command either River or passage, but if . . . there be a line of communication from the Castle to ye black mundings [Black Middens], it will be a place of great importance for commanding absolutely the mouth of ye River.' Beckman was responsible for designing Cliffords Fort at North Shields in 1672 which had much more effective control over the river.

By 1705-07 the castle was described as consisting of part regular and part irregular works 'after ancient manner,' but it was a good defence as it was situated on a peninsula and rock 80 feet (24m) perpendicular from the water. The land approach was by a regular hornwork and ditch not above 12 feet (3.6m) wide. It was recommended that the hornwork ditch should be widened to 60 feet (18.3m) and a counterscarp made after the modern method of fortifications. Parts of the old castle were to be lowered and good and useful batteries made in their place.

Fifty years later, the castle had an irregular wall and firing step along the cliffs. Towards the land was a strong wall and square tower with 'a kind of *fausse braye*,' a lower parapet at the foot of the rampart. There were rampart-mounted cannon at the salient angles. The small hornwork and ravelin (outworks) were still in existence at the entrance.

The castle was from time to time used for keeping French, Dutch and Swiss prisoners of war. In 1783-84 came the extensive alterations undertaken according to designs by Captain E Durnford. The gatehouse was fitted up for a barracks and nearly all the remaining monastic buildings were destroyed. The floor of the chapter house was dug up to make cellars for a regimental canteen. The Percy Chapel was converted into a powder magazine and remained so for forty years until restored by the architect, John Dobson. A few years later there were temporary barracks inside with a large ordnance storeroom. On the side of the castle next to the harbour and near the lighthouse was a battery for seven 18-pounder guns giving protection to shipping in the road. At the height of the Napoleonic Wars there were thirty-two 18-pounders, eight 12-pounders, and eleven 9-pounders.

By 1841 it was 'An old irregular work consisting of the ruins of a monastery and a castle with some modern works attached, situated on a projecting point of high land on the north of the entrance to the river Tyne.' The batteries held eighteen guns.

The construction of the north breakwater pier in 1854 by the River Tyne Commissioners led to quarrying on the south side of the castle and, with the driving of a roadway to the pier, removed much of the medieval walling on this side. In 1856 a trench was excavated on the landward side of the castle which altered the character of the approach and large powder magazines were built on the site of the cloister in 1863.

By 1881 Tynemouth had become an extensive work armed with twenty guns, of which six were modern rifled guns. This was the period when the commercial ports were officially recognised as places needing defence and two parts of the country in particular - the Firth of Forth and the Tyne - received much attention. In 1884 the Inspector General of Fortifications considered that the calibre of heavy guns need not exceed 9.2 inches (233mm) and that one of these and two of the medium guns proposed should be mounted in the Spanish Battery in order to obtain greater dispersion of the guns.

By 1893 emplacements for two 6 inch guns (152mm) had been constructed at the castle and the guns mounted on hydro-pneumatic disappearing carriages, replacing the miscellaneous scatter of earthen batteries for muzzle-loading artillery.

Twentieth-century defences
From 1900 until the outbreak of the First World War, two major considerations, technological and political, dominated the theory and practice of the nation's

defences. The first was the rationalisation of the types and calibres of coastal defence guns and their mountings. The second was the realisation that Germany and not France was now the main threat to Britain's naval supremacy and national security. This placed greater emphasis upon the defences of Britain' s east coast.

The gun batteries controlled by Tynemouth Castle, with those of the Firth of Forth, the Humber estuary and Harwich, had a vital role in protecting the commercial ports of the Northeast and its shipbuilding and armaments industry.

By 1905 the armament of Tynemouth consisted of one 9.2 inch Mark M BL, two 6 inch Mark VII BLs and two 12 pounder QFs. Following the demolition of Villiers's house in 1902, its site was occupied by three concrete buildings sheltered by a high earthen mound. The command block was of a single storey, but was flanked by two higher blocks carrying raised observation posts. The Command Post buildings survived intact until 1980, having been amalgamated within the Coastguard station which was built on the site piecemeal between about 1933 and about 1945.

This battery was further rehabilitated in 1914 when the Tyne entrance was designated as a Defended Port and the Tyne Fortress was extended well beyond Tynemouth itself. It remained operational and fully manned throughout the Second World War, when the emplacements were given concrete shelters as protection from aerial attack. The guns were removed in 1956.

Tynemouth Volunteer Artillery
It should be mentioned at this point that a volunteer artillery corps was founded at Tynemouth in 1805, but was disbanded at the end of the Napoleonic Wars in 1815. When another potential invasion threat

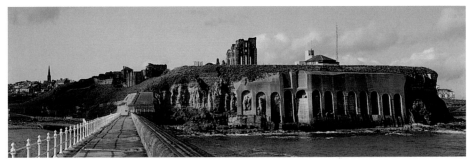

Headland from the north breakwater pier, showing coastal-erosion protection

arose in 1859 the (Tynemouth) First Northumberland Volunteer Artillery was formed - the first of its kind. In 1908, when the Territorial Force was created, this became the Tynemouth Royal Garrison Artillery (TF). In 1914 the Tyne Defences were manned by two regular companies of the Royal Garrison Artillery with the Territorials.

Lighthouse

Tynemouth had one of the earliest recorded monastic lighthouses. Mention is made in 1581/2 of 'a certaine order established for the kepinge of a continuall light in the night season at the easte ende of the churche of Tinmouthe Castle as in former times had been for the safegarde of such shippes as should passe by that coast.' This was a coal fire in an open brazier on the top of one of the two turrets flanking the east end of the presbytery.

It is probably thanks to its value as a navigational aid - a day mark - that the east end of the church was retained, virtually to its full height, after the dissolution of the priory. However, in 1659 the stairs leading to the top of the turret, where the brazier was, fell down.

There was great demand for another light and in 1664 Sir Edward Villiers had a new tower built and levied charges for its maintenance. This lighthouse was rebuilt

in 1775 and the coal brazier was replaced by an oil lamp with rotating reflectors in 1802. The lighthouse was transferred to Trinity House in 1840. When it was demolished in 1898, to be replaced by the lighthouses on St Mary's and Souter Points, nearly 200 carved stones derived from the priory ruins were found to have been built into it.

Coastal erosion, excavations, and repairs

Descriptions of coastal erosion affecting the walls occur as early as the fourteenth century. The concrete cliff-protection piers, so visible from the sea and the north pier, were built in the 1890s and are a manifestation of this continuing threat.

In 1904, the priory church came into the hands of the Office of Works. Excavations followed under the direction of W H Knowles in 1904-05. As more of the priory was taken out of military control, the claustral area was cleared in the early 1930s and the removal of the eighteenth-century barrack in the gatehouse followed the fire of 1936. Military occupation, however, continued until 1960, since when almost all traces have been removed from the interior and the medieval ruins have been displayed. The site has been in the care of English Heritage since 1984.

Glossary

Apse Semicircular or polygonal east end of a church

Aumbry Cupboard or recess in a wall for sacred vessels

Barbican Outer fortification protecting a gateway

Battery Platform or fortified work on or within which artillery is mounted

Blind arcading Line of arches on a solid wall for decoration

Buttresses Masonry projecting from a wall or the corner of a building to give additional strength or to resist the lateral thrust of an arch or roof

Capital Uppermost part of a column or shaft, often decorated

Chantry (chapel) Permanent endowment, usually expressed in a structure, for Mass to be said regularly for the spiritual welfare of a person or persons

Cloister Four-sided enclosure with a covered walk along each side; the centre of monastic life

Corbel Stone or wooden projection from a wall to support a beam, etc; corbel table, a projecting course of masonry serving as a support

Garth Area enclosed by a cloister

Gunport Opening in a wall though which a gun fires

Hoodmould Projecting horizontal moulding above a doorway or window to deflect rainwater

Machicolations Parapet carried on corbels and projecting from a wall face; the open spaces between the corbels enabled defenders to direct missiles on to attackers below

Ogee Double curve, one convex, the other concave; an arch composed of such curves

Orders Series of recessed arches and jambs forming a splayed opening

Pediment Low-pitched gable-end form used in a decorative rather than functional way above doors, windows, etc

Pilaster Shallow pier attached to a wall

Piscina Basin with a drain in a wall niche near the altar, for washing sacred vessels

Quire Part of a church between presbytery and pulpitum, containing stalls where monks sat to sing the Offices; choir

Reredos Ornamental screen behind and above an altar

Revetment Retaining wall built to support or hold back a mass of earth

Scalloped capital Capital decorated with a series of curves or scallops

Sedilia Stone seats for officiating clergy, recessed in the wall and often crowned with canopies, pinnacles, etc, on the south side of the presbytery near the altar

Spandrel Triangular area above the haunch of an arch; space between the shoulder of an arch and the surrounding mouldings

String course Horizontal band of masonry projecting from outer walls of a building and usually moulded

Tracery Decorative branching open stonework in the upper part of a Gothic window or archway

Trefoil Three lobed, e.g. tracery or panelling

Triforium Arcaded gallery between main arcade and clerestory